DEDICATION

To Coco and Noelle, who inspire me in every way.

To the entirety of the Czertak fam.

How to Befriend the World

Sophia Czertak

India | USA | UK

Presentation by *BookLeaf Publishing*

Web: www.bookleafpub.com

E-mail: info@bookleafpub.com

ISBN: 9789358315998

First edition 2024

ACKNOWLEDGEMENT

Anika Shandalov, my beautiful talented friend has made this book cover the meaningful art that it is. Anika is an illustrator and graphic designer, focused on telling stories through both traditional and digital media. A week prior to my publication, I had gone into a procrastinator's frenzy on a search for the perfect cover. Anika stepped in with two days and designed this with her heart and soul. I had told her I liked the idea of a young girl with a dog, and she gave me this piece. I admire her efficiency and craft. She's probably the reason you've picked this book up.

Benjamin Nakhuda, my roommate and collaborator in many ways. Ben took the time to take my author's portraits, putting his all into the set up. He is one of the most talented photographers I know, in addition to the colorful, unique stories he tells through his filmmaking.

The teachers and professors that have taught me everything I know. To Alan Theriault, who brought me into the poetry scene. He was my mentor from sixth grade through high school, when I'd participate in annual poetry reading competitions. To Derrick Ortega and Genevieve Kaplan, whose poetry classes have brought out many of the poems featured. I'm thankful for their notes and for introducing me to my many poetic inspirations, including them. To Mildred Lewis, who took the time to meet with me and discuss my poems in great detail in the midst of finals.

Noelle White, my roommate and best friend, who listens to me read every work of mine, even at their earliest and roughest stages. She is my creative muse, and I've had the pleasure of hearing her music production process as well as writing for one of her short films. May we always collaborate creatively and fuel one another's art.

Green, in all its Glory.

I smack my lips and spit, hoping sour gasoline could not infiltrate, through my nostrils and in my mouth, it's dry, my eyes are burning with lasting images. I've been looking the sun in the eye, now I am blind. For you, I'd drive the highways I always hated, I can't switch lanes and my tank is always running low. There's a gallon of premium in my backseat, and my windows are closed. I think I'd let my senses go, I think If I taste it I'll know

I've been poisoned.

In a closed pharmacy parking lot, I'll bathe in fumes. The poison has seeped into my tastebuds, I remember the first time. In a pharmacy parking lot, seven years old. I bit right in. I bit into glowing toxins, green and enticing. I always saw green as the color of love. How could love stick between my gums, underneath, and coat my throat? Still, I lay outside

Enveloped in green.

I lay in California grass, freshly coated in pesticides. My skin is bubbling, red, and covered in hives. I smack my lips and spit, watering chemical love with my envious regurgitations. I plant every seed that presses behind my teeth, yet never care to add dirt or water. Still, I smack my lips and spit, burying the tomato's body in a shallow grave. Many are growing now. Red and green. Green, red, red, green. Green spine, red body. Red was what I needed to taste. What everyone else calls love. I savor every juicy pairing, my lungs hydrated and supple.

I breathe in the open air.

Today I will walk. The gasoline spoils still linger behind the tip of my tongue. There is comfort in growth, there is comfort in care

And the lack thereof.

Remote Control

A face and a face and a face and a face
         Don't look at her like just some face
Face her
Learn a face, know a face, kiss a face,
Fuck a face
Leave the face
And always remember the face
See a face and a new face and an old face

See a face on the screen, know it is
Temporary. A naked body is nothing
But show biz, baby.
Eyes have memory.

Surf the channels, face the daze, tap on
information
So you know her name.

Spectate between dimension, pencil to paper,
greased
Fingers on the remote control. Lose your mind,
Lose your hands, close the door. Think with
something

New. Modernity shelters the beast, now boast

Your successes. Your deserving admiration.
Bodies.
Violence. Casting couch. Re-runs.

Again and again and again and again and again
Cut the cable.

Face yourself.

As You Wish

You only looked good through a memory
clogged cataract,

> my contact lens and
> licorice puddled gums

The scent of a rose garden at midnight,
something I could not fully see, but loved
how I now feel my wisdom teeth, I'm prodding
at their pain,
Forcing blood into its proper socket, and dirt
will find its place
in the remnants of the holes
in my mouth, adolescence stings
You sheltered me from the first and only bat I
have ever seen.
You sheltered me from becoming
 a day lady, a lady who flies, a lady who can see
at night, a lady
who can recognize the sting of a scorpion and
eat it.

Why do I wish to see at all, or to taste
everything that is bleak?

My gums make room for the leftover bacteria of
indulgence,

they bleed bubbling
pink wine stains

Walk with me
Smoke with me
Share with me,
the same cloud of human exhaust
in below zero winds.

I can't tell the difference between how my
fingers feel
And how yours feel lacing them

Maybe this is why I felt nothing when we
kissed.

Take me as a brutal gift, like everything you've
touched
I'll spend hours scrubbing your trace on my
inner thigh
And sobering my skin drunk, with my own tears
supple, sticky, smeared in snot,
                              wet cheeks cradled in
humidity
                              and the pocket of your
shoulder blade
                              something like a cavity

Don't talk sweet with me, I've got a toothache.

Just Like Me

I brush my teeth in tiny circles for the first time
          this week we have reached a
milestone
In our shared bathroom, before the mirror
her movements are my reflection
She plays a song I've never heard before, and
yet I know
          every lyric
drowns out my disarray, the way I gurgle and
spit
          how I choke on the mint
She coils her curls beside me, I get a whiff
Freshly showered hair and peach condensed
windows
sweet humidity

Femininity is a warm mold
growing in the walls, psilocybin
clinging to two lady beating hearts

The clock reads a time beyond its own mind
Six by eight, wet floors littered by our parallel
lives

My silhouette in the shower

Her silhouette in the shower

The earrings I left by the sink
Dangling just below her jaw

The pile of socks and the pile of shit
We open the window to let the light in

I Bet You Wouldn't Take Me
For a Coin Collector

You're tapping
your foot
impatiently, I've submitted
to a squat on the highway
Searching for quarters I mindlessly dropped
to the bottom of my bag, I'll pay
With a 1993 Montana, 1999 Kentucky, 2014
Maine.
I'll buy you an hour at the beach with four
quarters
 pertaining to no particular state.

You're watching the meter as Montana expires,
I'm sorting through napkins,
Receipts from an inebriated water,
nicotine, candy stripped, that candy's jacket.
The closets of lollipops, cough drops, three cake
pops, and a sandwich's sleeve.
Triple A, triple Target gift card. My best friend's
bra I've been meaning to return.

There's no time for us to grab a bite to eat, I
couldn't bare to let go of

Connecticut 2002, coated in some other guy's
chewing gum,
Stick it to tarnished Washington.

What's a meter apart from circulation,
who am I to hoard something remotely kin to
me.
I could spare ten minutes from this day,
Holding what has spent twenty-one years to get
a seat

In the bottom of my purse, I carry the Nutmeg
State.

Dish Dance

There are only so many dishes,
suds swarm and permeate perfervid pores
of the fingers that yearn to be torn and taunted,
eyed like
those in the popcorn ceiling, there are only so
many to count as the drain clogs,
and her eyes will leak sewage spills.

The spewing is slow and silent,
as directionless yet inherent as a newborn
with a gentle palm to its back.

This couldn't possibly be all we do
in this life, she needs so much more.
As far as counting goes, she could balance on
one leg, spinning,

only a 1,

2,

3,

4.

Her falling grace is the tendency to look up
as her knees buckle, she relies on
half-baked reasons
muddled in metal,
always at her disposal.

Rest Stops

I avoid break ups   like I've been taught   To
pass rest stops and push to the next Destination.
Looking back is harder than Planning a new
vacation.   If wealth had no limits   We would
never stop traveling. My father would Teach us
how to save and how to earn. How to
Get a job and   fucking learn.   I get what I Pay
for   and   I'm worth what I offer,   yet Money
is never spent on fuel. My mother collects Every
penny on the street, and when it's tails she Turns
it over. She makes a modest wage,   365 pennies
For 365 days.   I'd hold my piss and clench my
fist, My stomach wouldn't agree with the oil that
drenched my chicken tenders. All I'd Ever want
is tenders.   Be Tender with me now.
I'd beg for a pack of gum, one of   The impulse
buys I can't afford.   Still, I don't have   a few
dollars   on the floor, in my father's path and yet
I Didn't care   to ask, or even bother to think
That I didn't find it. We never find anything. It's
always "belongs to" and "courtesy of", and I'd
grow old and let My own body become
someone's To love. So I get my gasoline and
cheap watered down coffee and get my ass
Back on the road.

I   Move
         quickly
                    and   forget everything
I'm worried
about letting   go.

You Say I'm the Poet

Yet every time you pass a cactus with a flower
standing tall, you cannot help but ruminate
on the beauty that emerges from death. You told
me it's called a death bloom. The plant must die
to reproduce, and every flower rising above its
origin is a killer and a mother all in one.

Yet you ask me the same questions, not because
you forget, but because each time you are
hoping for a more interesting answer. So I strive
to be interesting to you.

Yet the Cassini space mission of 1997 makes
you cry uncontrollably. You say it was the first
to catch Saturn's rings, and lasted two decades.
It committed suicide in space. How can
something provide so much intellect and then
disappear in flames?

Yet you search every shoreline for rocks, and
only those that are green.

Yet you keep a box on your nightstand of all
your favorite tiny things. You reorganize your
box on a monthly basis, and you tell me the

story behind every object, so small. You keep a
clear box so they all can be seen: an elephant,
(your mother gifted you to remind you of your
first stuffed animal), a pearl (your therapist
gifted you, when you left for college), a small
playing card (just because it's cool), a dice, a
green rock found on an English beach, a bug in
resin, a scented wooden ball, a fake bear claw
(because it's immoral to have a real one), and a
real coyote claw (because you think they're just
like dogs).

Yet when I cry, you cry.

Yet you care for a black cat we found on the
street. You mop his piss, and feed him every day.
You carved a box the first night he slept in your
backyard. You set aside blankets and towels.
You cradle him, though you are deeply allergic.
You wear your love on the insides of your arms,
in puffy rashes.

Yet when you fall into a spiral, you count on
hope. You told me hope is the most important
thing. You find yourself so caught in helping
others, you forget to have hope in yourself.

Yet you love your home, and you love
mountains, because they make you feel small. In
a good way, you say.

Yet you admit you'll always love your mother
above any woman, even me.

The Mothers I have Yet to Meet

When I think of all the mothers I have yet to meet/and the lies they tell their sons about things that are sweet/I think of/why bees make honey, and why we think it's ours/why we plant annual seeds, because everything may die in the Winter but life goes on in Spring/why she checks the closet and under the bed, turns off the light and tells you to dream/why we send thank-you-letters for forgotten gifts, and give phone calls to distant relatives/why you should try every vegetable, it's nature's candy/why you can't pick the fruit just yet, even if you like the bitter taste of green/why we plant trees in the desert then call it a place to be/why you should wave at strangers, stop to chat with old friends in the grocery/why we extend a hand before the unfamiliar dog's nose/why you order from the kid's menu up until you're thirteen because even if you want a steak you're getting your last cheap grilled cheese/why when I meet her, she'll lie to him so he'll lie to me.

whMy I'mSO jPusHt fOiNIAe

The sound of every living person's footsteps.

Those that I can actively perceive, dragging their feet across my carpeted mind.

Those that I can imagine. Stomping, running, impatiently tapping and smacking

The lips. The string of saliva that joins two lips and the strings I imagine inside.

I can hear them, I can hear each string in a cacophonous concert I cannot digest

The coffee I drank at four in the afternoon laughing at me, I can hear through

The walls that act only as a barrier to my sight, the way they mock me

In my turtleneck sweater I promised myself I'd wear.

The promises I make and the pain of keeping
them.

The movement in my peripheral despite my need
for the world to be

Still, I sit in public space and I practice patience.

The sound of my own foot, my own throat
gulping it down

The echoes of life around me despite the
stillness of mine

There is Nothing Wrong

The worst of it all, she said, there was nothing
wrong.
She tilted her head to ease her untreated
swimmer's ear,
It was a pain that she would forget each day.

This is human nature,
her mother eased her anxious fertile mind.

To be the youngest child, to be her own vision of
the end,
she would lie in bed facing the wall for if
demons roamed
behind her, she would not look them in the eye.

Her stitched lip and her split right lobe, she
could not
decide between diet and regular coke.
It's all bad, it will all kill us.

She's a product of her own litter, she's one with
the overgrown garden
she wishes to see through her dusty window.

One day, neglect will be beautiful.

How to Befriend the World

Behave as gentle as your own love, lessen the
weight
on your knees. Bend down and wiggle your
fingers as
they long to kiss your wiggling toes. Go
wherever you can
fit, especially in nature. Lead with that heart,
embrace its impatience- not because it is bored,
it is overwhelmed
with excitement. There is so much to do
and you have the time so long as you allow it, if
you choose to

escape. Kick your feet in the air and rest your
head
in soft soil. Mesh your hair with the Earth's.
Feel your breath sink into hers. Watch your feet
sway
as they shift between blocking the light and
allowing it.
Remember that how you see them now, is how
they always look
up to you. If you haven't heard it today,
remember your own feet are always looking up
to you

engulfed in a pure white halo of light. Treat
above as below,
and never question why you stand where you
stand,
you can retrace your steps or you can
make new prints. Pick fruit so long as it has a
silky mouthfeel.
You may even pick fruits that are red,
even though everyone says to avoid red in
nature.

You're smart, and you know all things grown are
free.
Grow everything you can. Plant every seed
not in your teeth but in fresh soil,
wash your hair, read and write every day.

Make love
then make a new life of your own. Approach
conversation
with humor. Tell the gas station clerk you
appreciate them.
Run like a headless chicken
until the most appealing task or shiny object
calls your name.

Allow your hands to shake, your feet to tap.
Swim in the water you stumble upon.

Watch the bird that lands beside you
until it reaches the next neighborhood
and is but a mere spec. Watch everything
you can, until it changes. Watch the spider
that crawls on your stomach until it's between
your eyes. Spend money like your mother
and save it like your father, and know there is
balance
in what you give and get. You don't have to do
anything
 but love. Love will bring the opportunities you
dwell upon.

Who Knew Adults Could
Scrape Their Knees Too

Yesterday's fun is painted on its own page
A watercolor scrapbook draped across
my knees
Littered in blood coursing vines, someone ought
to water

            my

mind
I want a tattoo of my Sunday evening
bruise
I can model the pain of motion
My thin wrists bent by childlike design

     Yesterday I did a cartwheel for
     The first time.

New Year's Day

The yellow lines are consumed by movement
like vacuumed headaches after a night
Out. In the rolling frosted hills of January
Happiness trickles from Earth's glaciated
Eyes. In the light that reflects off of the snow
A glimmer of warmth, gleaming strands of hair
In a halo.
Metamorphic breakage of
Gold.

Kent Falls, January 1st.
Cracked lips bleed
on the scrapbook page. An image
Exposed by morning sun, a faint outline prevails
Through bare skeletons of trees. Life exists
In the movement. Shadows of dance,
Skipping pebbles in the running stream.

Cattle on the hill sound
out blurred memories.

Our Last Family Vacation

Ten years old in the backseat of our gold
        minivan cruising on the interstate,
windows down
Four kids cries drowning under the rippled wind
You could say this was bliss, my mother in the
passenger seat
periodically turning back
        in time

She has a kid to slash each tire so
We won't make it home
        But live on the shoulder of New
England
The Ford's been suffocated
in bubblegum, frayed polyester, stickers and torn
faux leather

She rips the stereo from its console with the
strength
of a mother, distressed

Veins bleeding hits of the eighties

She tosses the life out the window from the fast
lane

We press our noses to the glass and watch it
whimper

We listen for the wind but as the gold
locks in place, we are still, buckled
in one place

Dogs (Off the Leash)

Yesterday morning we had breakfast at the bar.
I ordered waffles and asked for a bite of your
eggs,
because I always regret a plate of sweet.

I haven't sat so high since I was a child.

They were brothers, cared for, and happy
in one another's company, well fed but eternally
hungry,
cravings unsatiated by the tug of a leash.

Their hair was well-kept and groomed regularly,
bones cushioned in a layer of love, as if being
handled
by the bigger man discredited the desire to be
free.

They left their kibble in both bowls as I
left the waffles on the plate, and took everything
you had.
You signed the check as I begged to leave, and I
did,
silently.

Coco/Dollar Slice

I'd like to eat a pizza in every city, with you
these daily tasks have meaning

You pick up
loose hubcaps, me and you
march around with our angst and music

You say it's how you get out of bed and
each morning I'm inhaling something
you rolled, on the floor laughing

You make my stomach hurt in a good way,
a kind of ache that lingers, you
feel it with me, my bones are old

We don't move much but we love to travel,
We love the new
talk we share over a coffee,
sometimes I cover, sometimes you do
hold my hand in a crowd, anxiety has her
hold on me and you, enabling

We yell in the street, get out of our town!
We rule, we judge, we gossip, then eat
sandwiches and art, cartoons and

two-player fun

We play the games I never did
as a child I was missing someone
curious
to see what we do next,
first let's check every pizza off our list

Being a Kid on Sunday

She was counter-height when she asked for a
strawberry frosted donut
and promised she would eat it all, because a
dollar for a donut was
a price she could not fully understand, but she
trusted her father's word
when he warned the precautions of wasting a
single.

She had a carefully constructed methodology to
proper indulgence,
her small thumb under the soft breading, she
would hold it close,
brushing her self-cut bangs aside to eye each
fiber as she pulled and
prioritized sweetness, always the icing last. Her
fingers were coated and stuck
to the pew as they marched along the rim,
pestering gray heads
to the beat of the sermon.

Her breath was warm and cavity prone, and
she'd wait for after mass
when she'd sit on her grandfather's lap at the
head of the table.

On their shared birthday, they wore matching
shirts.

He was a pug-faced man,
always wearing a muted flannel.
They were cigar soaked, and never let go of
the acidity of his daily pasta sauce. The dust
accumulated
on his flannel just as it did in the dirt basement
of his seventeenth century home. He smelled
like mothballs
and tobacco, garlic and tomato. He smelled like
red wine
for good health, and
dark chocolate on occasion.

When she could see over the counter, she no
longer fit in any lap
and lacked a lap to fit in, anyway.

Her appetite exceeded a dollar, so her father
brought weekly business
to the gas station, where she'd get a lottery ticket
and even if she lost
she gained a penny.

And that shirt still hangs in her closet, smeared
in
snot and sprinkles, cigars and scratched luck.

Killdeer

Maybe sleep is a bandaid to delusion
I know every bird feels it and that is why they
leave
I feel less alone with them, though I'll never see
a repeat
They tell me how to feel
until they subside
stationary, as stars that swallow me

The manic moon is telling me they're still my
friends.
And the night, something of a siren, sings her
song and
lets me dream
we are all still in love

I forgive everyone, expecting some in change
If only it came first
in our long sequence of human emotion

I'm tired of being the woman that I am
I don't want it to be easy,
Where would my purpose go?
I love being the creator of my own problems,
At least I am in control

Forget the Olive Branch

My outer shell is an olive hue, thick and
moldable, so I adorn it
in the surrendered jewels
of whom I hold no memory.

My body is a green fruit, latching to its branch
They do not want the skin, it's been picked at.
The body has fallen before, and they glued it
back.

Every inked in pattern,
strangers tip-toe around their given thighs.
The people I've loved
have touched me all over and
again, I felt nothing
when my thoughts fell down my spine.
How long would it take to erase
these designs?

I've never tasted my own flesh, yet
as I peel back, my yearning is insistent.
I am raw. I am new. And it's all for you.
I want to be pink, coursing with blood.
I want to pluck at the roots of this life,
My scattered network of budding promises,

Might it be sweeter with you?
Do your veins carry more than they can provide?
Should we empty them, relieve their undying
pride?

You've set me here to burn, teased
with leathery injuries.
You're touch is sunlight, concentrated on
catching my glass eyes.

Do you expect anything to grow
in an orchard on fire?

Red (in all its reverence)

pick the tomatoes
lay beside me, land on my sheets,
the first ladybug I see in Spring

stand beside me in the mirror
we'll laugh and we'll sing

something about looking your reflection in the
eyes
is more intimate than cheek to cheek

there is eternal grace in women laying
red as can be